Contents

Some words are shown in bold, **like this**. You can find out what they mean by looking in the glossary.

At the surface

A pond is a small area of **fresh water**. A pond is a type of **habitat** where some animals find **shelter** or food. Some animals live on or visit the surface of a pond.

Please return/renew this item
by the last date shown.
Books may also be renewed by
phone and Internet.

Louise Spilsbury

company incorporated in England and Wales having its registered office at 7 Pilgrim Street, London, EC4V 6LB – Registered company number: 6695582

www.raintree.co.uk
myorders@raintreepublishers.co.uk

Edited by Rebecca Rissman, Dan Nunn, and John-Paul Wilkins
Designed by Steve Mead
Original illustrations © Capstone Global Library Ltd 2013
Illustrations by Gary Hanna
Picture research by Ruth Blair
Production by Alison Parsons
Originated by Capstone Global Library Ltd
Printed and bound in China

ISBN 978 1 406 25128 9 (hardback)
16 15 14 13 12
10 9 8 7 6 5 4 3 2 1

ISBN 978 1 406 25135 7 (paperback)
17 16 15 14
10 9 8 7 6 5 4 3 2 1

British Library Cataloguing in Publication Data
Spilsbury, Louise.
Look inside a pond.
577.6'3-dc23
A full catalogue record for this book is available from the British Library.

We would like to thank the following for permission to reproduce photographs: Alamy pp. 14 (© Terry Whittaker), 27 (© FLPA); Corbis p. 28 (© */Design Pics); Naturepl pp. 15, 23 (© Stephen Dalton), 17 (© Frei / ARCO), 20 (© GEOFF DORE), 24 (© Jane Burton), 25 (© Kim Taylor), 26 (© Paul Hobson); Photoshot p. 21 (© NHPA); Shutterstock pp. 5 (© optimarc), 6 (© Elenaphotos21), 7 (© Stargazer), 8 (© Ron Rowan Photography), 9 (© Andreas Altenburger), 11 (© Naas Rautenbach), 12 (© bluecrayola), 13 (© Uryadnikov Sergey), 18 (© Andreas G. Karelias), 19 (© Laurie L. Snidow), 29 (© formiktopus).

Cover photograph of common frog (*Rana temporaria*), also known as the European Common Frog, reproduced with permission of Shutterstock (© Uryadnikov Sergey).

We would like to thank Michael Bright and Diana Bentley for their invaluable help in the preparation of this book.

Every effort has been made to contact copyright holders of any material reproduced in this book. Any omissions will be rectified in subsequent printings if notice is given to the publisher.

Disclaimer
All the internet addresses (URLs) given in this book were valid at the time of going to press. However, due to the dynamic nature of the internet, some addresses may have changed, or sites may have changed or ceased to exist since publication. While the author and publisher regret any inconvenience this may cause readers, no responsibility for any such changes can be accepted by either the author or the publisher.

Pond skaters are **insects** that can run on water! Their long legs help them to skate on the top of ponds. They use their short front legs to catch small insects to eat.

▲ Tiny hairs on the pond skater's legs stop it from falling through the surface of the water.

A duck is a bird that has **webbed feet** to help it swim. It swims to find plants, snails, frogs, and other small animals to eat. It also sticks its head under water to find food in the mud.

webbed feet

You can tell ▶ this mallard duck is a **male** because it has a green head.

▲ Mother ducks show babies where to find food.

Female ducks make **nests** of grass and feathers near ponds. They lay their eggs inside the nest. The baby ducks that **hatch** out of the eggs can swim straight away.

Dragonflies fly faster than any other **insects**. They can also **hover** in one spot over a pond, like a helicopter. Their huge eyes look all around to find flies and other insects to eat.

▼ This dragonfly is on the lookout for food.

Female dragonflies lay eggs on pond plants. The young that **hatch** from the eggs live under water and eat small fish and insects. Later they climb up tall plants by the edge of the pond and change into adults.

This dragonfly ▶ has just changed into an adult.

On the bank

Some animals live on or in the muddy **bank** next to the pond. Other animals visit the bank to eat the animals that live there.

Herons are grey birds with long legs. They stand very still by the pond and watch for food. Herons stab the water to catch fish and frogs in their beaks.

▲ A long, sharp beak is great for catching fish!

Frogs are **amphibians**. They live on land but lay their eggs in water. **Tadpoles** that **hatch** from the eggs have tails to swim. They live and feed on plants under water.

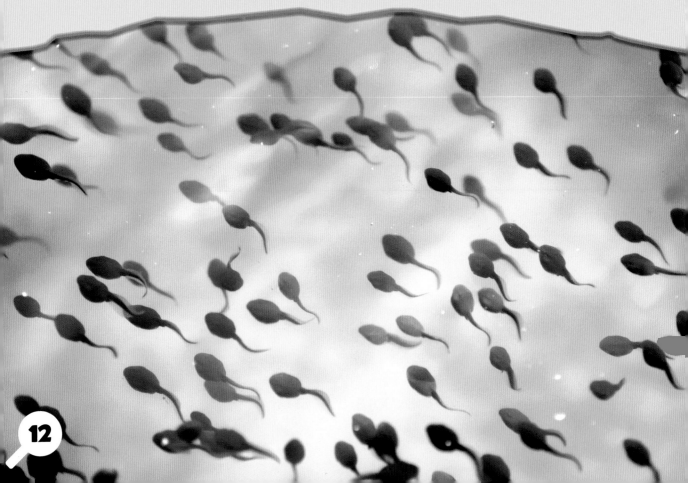

▼ These tadpoles have recently hatched.

▲ This adult frog is fully grown.

Tadpoles grow into frogs. Their tails shrink and they grow legs so they can hop out of the pond. Frogs catch flies and other small animals to eat on the pond edge using their long, sticky tongues.

Water shrews dig short tunnels into the **bank**. They make warm **nests** inside for their babies from leaves and sticks. Water shrews hide in tunnels to escape birds and fish that try to eat them!

▼ Water shrews are about as long as a pencil.

▲ Big, hairy feet help water shrews to dive.

Water shrews leave their tunnels to dive for food. The stiff hairs that cover their back feet help them to swim. They catch pond **insects** and small fish using their sharp, pointy teeth.

In the water

Some animals live under water in the pond for most or all of the time. They swim about and catch all the food they need in the water.

Pike are big, fierce fish with sharp teeth. They hide among pond plants and dart out quickly to catch **prey** that swims past. Pike eat fish, frogs, ducklings, and water shrews.

▲ Big eyes help pike to spot prey!

Terrapins are small turtles that live in ponds. They kick their **webbed feet** to swim about. Terrapins have a hard mouth like a beak that snaps up fish, plants, and **tadpoles**.

▼ Terrapins can eat and sleep under water.

▲ Terrapins like to warm up in the sun.

Terrapins can stay in the water for days but they often climb out on to rocks or logs to warm up in the sunlight. If there is not much space they may lie on top of each other! Terrapins also lay their eggs on land.

The diving beetle spends most of its time under water. It comes to the surface to collect air bubbles under its wing covers. It uses this air to breathe when it dives and swims.

▼ Diving beetles are great swimmers.

▲ This diving beetle is munching a tadpole.

Diving beetles dart quickly through water looking for food. They move their hairy back legs like paddles to swim along. The beetles have large **jaws** to catch and eat fish and **tadpoles**.

Muddy bottom

The bottom of a pond can be muddy and dark. It is a good place to hide from **predators** and to lay eggs.

Caddis fly eggs **hatch** under water. The young caddis flies are like little caterpillars. They make cases around themselves from sand, shells, and bits of plant. The cases protect their soft bodies.

▲ A case of shells is a safe place to hide!

Small stickleback fish have sharp spines sticking up on their backs. These make it hard for herons, water shrews, and other **predators** to swallow them! Sticklebacks eat worms, **insects**, eggs, and small fish.

▼ Sticklebacks are a tricky meal for many fish!

spine

▲ The male makes a nest from plants and stones.

Male sticklebacks make **nests** at the bottom of the pond. The **female** lays eggs inside the nest. The male chases off any animals that try to eat the eggs.

Crayfish hide under stones in the day and creep out at night to catch food. Crayfish have ten legs for walking quickly across a pond floor.

▼ Crayfish have tough shells and big claws.

claw

fish

▲ Crayfish are not fussy eaters!

Crayfish use their giant claws to catch and hold food. They eat snails, **insects**, fish, eggs, and almost anything else they can find on the muddy bottom!

Pond habitats

In summer, pond water is warm and there are many plants. Many animals are in the pond. In winter, ponds are cold and there are fewer plants. Fewer animals are in the pond.

▼ A pond in summer.

▲ A pond in winter.

Ponds are great places to spot animals. Sit and watch them come and go, but remember:
- Even shallow water can be dangerous, so take care near the edge of a pond.
- Do not remove plants or animals from ponds because they may not survive away from them.

Glossary

amphibian type of animal that begins life in water and then lives on land for part of its life. Newts, frogs, and toads are types of amphibian.

bank ground at the edge of a river or stream

female sex of an animal or plant that is able to produce eggs or seeds. Females are the opposite sex to males.

fresh water water in rivers, ponds, and many lakes that is not salty like seawater

habitat place where particular types of living things are likely to live. For example, polar bears live in snowy habitats and camels live in desert habitats.

hatch come out of an egg

hover stay hanging in the air

insect type of small animal that has three body parts, six legs, and usually wings. Ants and dragonflies are types of insect.

jaw part of an animal's mouth used to grip, chew, or bite

male sex of an animal or plant that is unable to produce eggs or seeds. Males are the opposite sex to females.

nest place where a bird or other animal lays eggs or cares for its young. Nests are often made from twigs or grass.

predator animal that hunts and catches other animals for food

prey animal that is caught and eaten by another animal

shelter place that provides protection from danger or bad weather

tadpole young stage in a frog's life cycle. Tadpoles live under water before changing into frogs.

webbed feet feet with skin stretched between the toes that animals, such as ducks and frogs, use to help them swim

Find out more

Books

Minibeasts in a Pond (Where to Find Minibeasts), Sarah Ridley (Franklin Watts, 2010)

Ponds (Nature Trails), Anita Ganeri (Raintree, 2011)

RSPB First Book of Pond Life, Derek Niemann (A & C Black, 2012)

Websites

Explore pond habitats and do a virtual pond dip at:
http://www.naturegrid.org.uk/pondexplorer/pondexplorer.html

See videos of ponds and lakes and animals that live in them at:
http://www.bbc.co.uk/nature/habitats/Lake

Discover more about pond life at:
http://www.enchantedlearning.com/biomes/pond/pondlife.shtml

Index

Science Keywords

THE MATERIAL WORLD

Karen Bryant-Mole

WAYLAND

Titles in the series

English Keywords – Words and Sentences
Maths Keywords – Numbers and Calculations
Science Keywords – The Living World
Science Keywords – The Material World

find Wayland on the Internet at http://www.wayland.co.uk

All Wayland books encourage children to read and help them improve their literacy.

✓ The contents page, page numbers, headings and index help children find specific pieces of information.

✓ The layout of the book helps children understand and use alphabetically ordered texts.

✓ The design of the book helps children scan text to locate particular key words.

✓ The structure of the book helps children understand and use non-fiction texts that are made up of definitions and explanations.

If a particular key word has an unusual plural form or appears in a modified form within the text of the book, this form has been shown in brackets.

Consultant: Stuart Ball

Design: Jean Wheeler
Cover design: Viccari Wheele

First published in 1999 by Wayland Publishers Limited,
61 Western Road, Hove, East Sussex BN3 1JD

© Copyright 1999 BryantMole Books

British Library Cataloguing in Publication Data

Bryant Mole, Karen
Science Keywords – The Material World. – (Keywords)
1. Materials – Dictionaries, Juvenile literature
I. Title
570.3

ISBN 07502 2421 5

Printed and bound in Italy by Eurografica S.p.a.

Acknowledgements
The publishers would like to thank the following for allowing their pictures to be reproduced in this book.
(t) = top (b) = bottom
Zul Mukhida: 4(t); 5(t); 6 both(b); 9(t); 12(t); 15(t); 18 (b); 19(b); 20(t); 21(b); 23(b); 25(b); 27(t); 28(b); 29(b); 30(both); 31(b)
Positive Images: 6(t); 11(b); 15(b); 23 (t); 24(b)
Tony Stone Images: 4(b) Ken Fisher; 5(b) Peter Cade; 7(t) Howard Kingsnorth; 7(b) Nicholas DeVore; 8(t) Jess Stock; 8(b) Rau Massey; 9(b) ESA/K Horgan; 10(t) Ralph H Wetmore; 12(b) Darryl Torckler; 13(t) Oli Tennent; 13(b) G Ryan and S Beyer; 14(t) Karl Weatherly; 14(b) Jon Riley; 16(t) Ken Graham; 16(b) David Madison; 17(t) Lori Adamski Peek; 18(t) Stephen Johnson; 20(b) Michael Rosenfeld; 21(t) Paul Harris; 25(t) Chad Ehlers; 28(t) Michael Busselle; 29(t) David Frazier; **Wayland Publishers Limited:** 10(b); 11(t); 17(b); 19(t); 22(t); 22(b); 24(t); 26(t); 26(b); 27(b); 31(t)

Contents

How to use this book

This book is made up of key words. Each key word is printed in **bold** and is followed by an explanation.

• The key words are listed in alphabetical order. The words printed in large letters at the top of the page will help you find the key word you are looking for. The word at the top of each left-hand page is the first key word that appears on that page. The word at the top of each right-hand page is the last key word that appears on that page. Every key word that comes in between these two words can also be found on these two pages.

• You will find an index at the back of the book. The index will show you where the explanation of each key word can be found, other pages where that word appears and where you can find any related pictures.

• As you read through an explanation, you will notice that some of the words may be underlined. Each of these underlined words has its own explanation.

Enjoy exploring the Keywords trail!

absorb

a

absorb Take in moisture, energy, light or heat.

accelerate Move faster or speed up. Objects accelerate as a result of forces, for example gravity, working on them.

air Air is all around us. It is made up of a mixture of gases. The warmer the air, the more space it takes up and the lighter it becomes. Warm air always rises. (See also air resistance, insulator, sound and water cycle.)

▲ This balloon is full of **air**.

air resistance Also called drag. A type of force caused by friction between the air and an object moving through it. Air resistance makes the object slow down, or decelerate.

alloy A metal that is made of two or more metals that have been mixed together. Bronze, for instance, is an alloy of tin and copper.

ammeter An instrument that is used to measure electric current.

appearance What something looks like.

artificial Not natural. It often describes something that is meant to look or act like a natural object or material, such as an artificial flower or artificial silk.

▲ **Air resistance** is slowing this sky diver down.

attract Pull towards. When a magnet pulls another magnet or a magnetic object towards it, it is said to be attracting that object. Two magnets will attract each other if they have different poles facing each other. (See also repel.)

b

balanced forces See force.

battery (batteries) Batteries store chemical energy. When a battery becomes part of an electrical circuit the chemical energy in it is changed by a chemical reaction to electricity. (See also cell.)

beam A band of light, made up of rays.

boil Heat a liquid to a temperature at which bubbles of gas start to be formed. The bubbles of gas rise up to the surface and burst. The exact temperature at which a liquid starts to boil is called its boiling point.

bounce Hit something and spring back.

brakes Brakes are used to stop or slow down a moving object. Brakes usually work by causing friction.

bulb See light bulb.

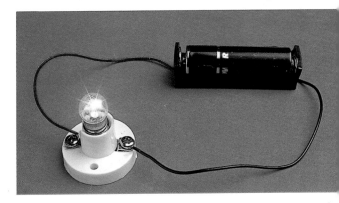

▲ This **battery** is part of an electrical circuit.

▲ Cables attached to the handlebars of this bike are linked to its **brakes**.

cable

cable A bundle of <u>wires</u>, often with an <u>electrical</u> <u>insulator</u> around it.

cell An object made up of two different <u>metals</u> in particular liquids. A cell can produce an <u>electric</u> <u>current</u>. <u>Batteries</u> are made up of cells.

Celsius A <u>scale</u> of <u>temperature</u>. Water <u>freezes</u> at 0 degrees Celsius and <u>boils</u> at 100 degrees Celsius. (See also <u>Fahrenheit</u>.)

chemical energy A type of <u>potential</u> <u>energy</u>. It is stored in things like <u>fuels</u>, food and <u>batteries</u>. The energy is released and changed by <u>chemical</u> <u>reactions</u>. Chemical reactions can, for instance, change the chemical energy in wood to <u>heat</u>, in batteries to electricity and in food to <u>kinetic energy</u>.

▲ The **chemical energy** in the wood is being changed to heat.

chemical reaction A changing of one or more <u>substances</u> into new substances. A cake, for example, is a result of a chemical reaction. Its ingredients are changed when they are mixed together and heated. <u>Energy</u> is usually needed to start a chemical reaction. Most chemical reactions are <u>irreversible</u>.

▲ Cake mixture is changed into a cake by **chemical reaction**.

circuit A loop around which an electric current can flow. The current usually flows along a wire or wires. The loop must include a source of electricity, such as a battery. It might also include things such as switches and light bulbs.

compass An instrument with a pointer, or needle, which points to the north. It is used for showing direction. The needle is a magnet.

complete Make whole. Finish off.

compress Make smaller, usually by squeezing or pressing.

condensation Material that has been condensed. Often used to describe the droplets of water on the inside of cold windows or on a bathroom mirror.

condense Cool a gas to a temperature at which it turns into a liquid.

conduct Allow heat, sound or electric current to pass through.

conductor A material that allows heat, sound or electric current to pass through it easily.

▲ A **compass** is used to show direction.

▲ There is **condensation** on this window.

connector

connector Anything that joins two parts of an <u>electrical</u> <u>circuit</u>.

current See <u>electric current</u>.

current electricity See <u>electricity</u>.

darkness Little or no <u>light</u>.

day Either, a 24 hour period of time, or, the time of <u>light</u> between sunrise and sunset. (See also <u>Earth</u> and <u>night</u>.)

decelerate <u>Move</u> more slowly, or slow down. Objects decelerate as a result of <u>forces</u>, for example <u>friction</u>, working on them. (See also <u>brakes</u>.)

density (dense) To do with the <u>mass</u> and <u>volume</u> of something. Dense <u>materials</u> can be thought of as weighing a lot for their size.

direction The particular path, or way, taken by a <u>moving</u> object. Or, the way that something is pointing, for example, north.

displacement (displace) The taking away or pushing away of a <u>material</u>, especially a <u>liquid</u>, by something else which takes its place.

▲ Skiers ski in a downhill **direction**.

▲ This stone is **displacing** water.

dissolve Completely mix a solid or a gas into a liquid.

dull Also called matt (or mat). Not bright. The opposite of shiny. A dull material does not reflect light very well.

▲ The paint in this paintpot is made up of a powder **dissolved** in water.

Earth The planet on which we live. The Earth orbits the Sun. It takes about one year to complete one orbit. The Earth also rotates. It takes a day to make one complete turn. As it rotates, it turns to face towards or away from the Sun. This gives us day and night. (See also gravity and Moon.)

electric charge Everything is made up of small parts called atoms. Atoms contain two different particles called protons and electrons. Materials are usually made up of atoms that contain the same number of protons and electrons. However, when two materials are rubbed together, electrons can move from one to the other. When an atom has a different number of electrons to protons, it is said to be charged, or to have an electric charge.

▲ The **Earth** is a planet.

electric current

electric current A movement of electric charge. Sometimes called a flow of electricity. Electric current is measured in amps.

electrical To do with electricity.

electricity To do with electric charge. Electricity is a type of energy. It is a very useful type of energy as it can easily be changed into other forms of energy, such as heat, sound or light. There are two main forms of electricity: static electricity and current electricity. Static electricity means electric charges that stay in one place. Lightning is a result of static electricity that has built up in storm clouds.
Current electricity means electric charges that are always moving. It is this type of electricity that is most useful to us because it can be moved to wherever it is needed. Batteries produce current electricity. Power stations also produce current electricity.
This is sent to businesses and homes to make things such as light bulbs and electrical machines work. This type of current electricity is known as mains

▲ Lightning is a result of static **electricity**.

▼ Current **electricity** is made in power stations.

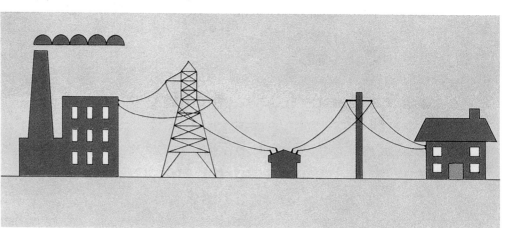

electricity. Mains electricity can be very dangerous. As well as flowing through wires, it can also flow through people. NEVER play with plugs and sockets. (See also conductor, electric current and insulator.)

electromagnet A magnet that has been made by passing an electric current through a coil of wire. Electromagnets are useful because they can be switched on and off. The strength of the magnet can be changed by changing the strength of the electric current.

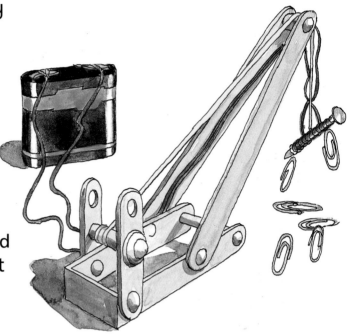

▲ Here is a simple **electromagnet**.

energy Things need energy in order to work or do work. It is what makes things 'go'. There are many different types of energy, such as kinetic energy, potential energy and chemical energy. Electricity, heat, sound and light are also forms of energy. Energy cannot be made nor can it be used up but it can be changed from one type to another. A hairdryer, for instance, does not use up electricity, it just changes it into heat. Energy is measured in joules.

evaporate Change from a liquid to a gas, but without reaching boiling point. All liquids slowly evaporate. The warmer the air and the faster the flow of air around the liquid, the faster it will evaporate.

▲ The water will **evaporate** from this wet washing.

fabric

f

fabric A <u>material</u> that is usually made by weaving or knitting <u>fibres</u>. Clothes, curtains and sheets are all made from fabric. Fabric is usually <u>soft</u> and can be cut and sewn.

Fahrenheit A <u>scale</u> of <u>temperature</u>. Water <u>freezes</u> at 32 degrees Fahrenheit and <u>boils</u> at 212 degrees Fahrenheit. (See also <u>Celsius</u>.)

fibre A thread, often of a type that can be woven to make <u>fabric</u>. Also used to describe any long, thin, thread-like object.

filter Pass a <u>liquid</u> through a <u>material</u> such as paper. Any <u>insoluble</u> <u>solids</u> in the liquid will be trapped by the filter paper.

flexible Can bend or be bent. Not <u>rigid</u>.

float Be held up by <u>air</u> or, more usually, by a <u>liquid</u>, such as <u>water</u>. When an object is placed in water, it <u>displaces</u> some water to make room for itself. The water that has been pushed away pushes back, trying to get back into the space it was in. If the water pushes back strongly enough to hold up the object, the object will float. If not, it will <u>sink</u>. The larger the <u>surface</u> of the object,

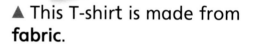

▲ This T-shirt is made from **fabric**.

▲ When something is held up by water, it is said to **float**.

the more there is for the water to push against and the more likely it is to float. The denser the material the object is made from, the less likely it is to float.

fluid Able to flow and spread everywhere. Liquids and gases are fluids.

force A push or pull. Forces can make an object move or stop. They can change the speed or direction of a moving object. They can squash or stretch an object.
There are many types of forces, including magnetic force, friction and gravity.
When forces act in the same direction on an object, that object moves at a speed which stays the same. When forces of the same strength act in opposite directions on an object, that object stays still and does not move. The forces are said to be balanced. Balanced forces are rather like two tug-of-war teams pulling with the same strength on a rope. The rope does not move.
All forces are measured in newtons. (See also air resistance and weight.)

freeze (freezing) Cool a liquid to a temperature at which it turns into a solid, or is frozen. The exact temperature at which a liquid freezes is called its freezing point.

▲ The wind can act as a **force**. It is pushing this yacht's sails.

▲ When water **freezes** it turns to ice.

friction

friction A type of <u>force</u>. Friction is a force that happens when two <u>materials</u> rub together. It makes objects slow down, or <u>decelerate</u>. The <u>rougher</u> the <u>surface</u> of the objects, the more friction there is and the more difficult it is for them to slide over each other. The <u>smoother</u> the surface, the less friction there is and the more easily the objects will slide. As the two objects rub against each other, some of their <u>kinetic energy</u> is changed into <u>heat</u>.

fuel A <u>material</u> that, when burnt, changes <u>chemical energy</u> into other forms of <u>energy</u>, such as <u>heat</u>. Coal is a type of fuel.

fulcrum See <u>lever</u>.

g

gas One of the three <u>states of matter</u>. Gas has no particular shape. The amount of space it takes up can change. Most gases have no colour or smell. Gases are <u>fluids</u>. <u>Air</u> is made up of a mixture of different gases. (See also <u>invisible</u>.)

gravity A type of <u>force</u>. Gravity is a force that pulls all objects together. The <u>Earth</u> is very big and its gravity is very strong. It pulls everything down

▲ Skate blades are smooth and thin, so there is as little **friction** as possible.

▲ Cars need a **fuel**, such as petrol or diesel.

towards itself. The Earth's gravity also pulls the Moon towards it and keeps the Moon orbiting around it. The Sun's gravity keeps the Earth orbiting around the Sun. (See also potential energy and weight.)

h

▲ Hairdryers give out **heat**.

hard Does not give when touched or pressed. The opposite of soft.

heat A type of energy that flows from a hotter object to a colder object. Heat from a bowl of hot soup would flow into the colder air that surrounds it, making the soup cool down. Dark-coloured materials absorb more heat than light-coloured materials. People often wear light-coloured clothes in the summer because light colours, especially white, reflect heat. (See also conductor, friction and insulator.)

i

insoluble Cannot be dissolved.

instrument An object that helps you do something.

▲ Sand is **insoluble**.

insulator

insulator A <u>material</u> that stops or slows the flow of <u>heat</u>, <u>sound</u> or <u>electric current</u> through it. Many <u>plastics</u> are good <u>electrical</u> insulators. They are used to make electrical <u>machines</u> safe to use. Trapped <u>air</u> is a good sound and heat insulator. Double glazed windows have trapped air between the two layers of glass. This keeps heat in and sound out. Insulators can also be used to keep heat out. Foam, which holds trapped air, is used in cool bags. It helps to keep any food and drink in the bag cold.

invisible Cannot be seen. Most <u>gases</u> are invisible.

iron A type of <u>metal</u>. Iron is <u>magnetic</u> and is a good <u>conductor</u> of <u>electric current</u>.

irreversible Cannot change, or be changed, back to the way it was.

kinetic energy A type of <u>energy</u> that all <u>moving</u> things have. You can tell that a moving object has energy because if it hits an object something happens. If a hammer hits a nail, for instance, it makes the nail move. (See also <u>friction</u>.)

▲ The polar bear cub's fur acts as an **insulator**.

▲ This golf ball has **kinetic energy**.

l

lens A piece of glass, or other transparent material, with one or two curved surfaces. Lenses are used to bend rays of light. There are two main types of lens. A convex lens curves outwards. It makes things look bigger. A concave lens curves inwards. It makes things look smaller. Lenses are used in spectacles, magnifying glasses, cameras, microscopes and telescopes. You also have a lens in each eye.

lever A bar that rests on a turning point called a pivot or fulcrum. It can be used to lift or move an object. This idea is used in objects like pliers and wheelbarrows. The lever is a type of simple machine.

light A type of energy. Light comes from the Sun and from other objects such as candles and light bulbs. Light travels in straight lines. It can travel through transparent and translucent materials but reflects off opaque materials. Shiny, smooth materials reflect a lot of light. Dull materials absorb more light and reflect less light. Light looks as though it has no colour but is actually made up of a spread of colours, called a spectrum. (See also luminous.)

▲ The **lens** in a magnifying glass makes things look bigger.

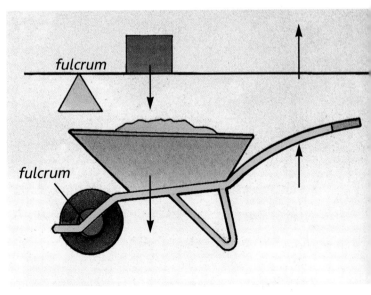

fulcrum

fulcrum

▲ A wheelbarrow is a type of **lever**.

light bulb

light bulb Inside a light bulb there is a thin <u>wire</u>, called a filament. When an <u>electric current</u> flows through the filament it heats up and gives out a white <u>light</u>. Light bulbs are <u>luminous</u>.

liquid One of the three <u>states of matter</u>. Liquids are <u>fluids</u>. They can take the shape of whatever they are put in. Although a liquid's shape might change, its <u>volume</u> does not.

loop A <u>complete</u> <u>circuit</u>, or path, which <u>electric current</u> can <u>flow</u> around.

luminous Is able to give out <u>light</u>. Candles, televisions and torches can all be luminous.

m

machine Anything that makes a job easier to do. It includes objects that are not usually thought of as being machines, such as wheelbarrows, as well as objects like washing machines and vacuum cleaners. Many machines are made up of lots of simple machines connected together. Simple machines include the <u>lever</u>, the <u>ramp</u>, the <u>screw</u> and the <u>pulley</u>.

magnet A <u>metal</u> that other magnets and some other metals are <u>attracted</u> to. The

▲ The filament inside this **light bulb** is glowing.

▲ Candles are **luminous**.

stronger the magnet, the greater its magnetic force. (See also compass, electromagnet, iron, magnetic, magnetise, magnetic field and pole.)

magnetic A way of describing something that is attracted to a magnet.

magnetic field The area around a magnet in which its magnetic force works. The stronger the magnet, the greater its magnetic force and the larger its magnetic field. Because magnets have a magnetic field, they can attract magnetic materials through non-magnetic materials such as air, water or fabric.

magnetic force A type of force that pulls magnetic materials in towards a magnet and causes two magnets to attract or repel each other.

magnetise Make something into a magnet. When something that is made from a magnetic material touches a magnet, it too becomes a magnet and will attract other magnetic materials. When it stops touching the magnet, it stops being a magnet. Things that are only magnetised for a short time are called temporary magnets. Anything that is a magnet all the time is called a permanent magnet.

▲ This drawing shows a magnet's **magnetic field**.

▼ These paper clips have been **magnetised**.

magnetism

magnetism Another name for magnetic force.

mains electricity See electricity.

manufactured An object or material made by people or machines.

mass To do with how much there is of something. Although the weight of something can change depending on how strong the pull of gravity is, its mass always stays the same. Mass is measured in kilograms. (See also weigh.)

material What things are made of, or from.

measure (measuring) Find the size or amount of something.

melt Heat a solid to a temperature at which it becomes a liquid. The exact temperature at which a solid melts is called its melting point.

metal Any one of a group of materials that includes gold, silver, iron and copper. Metals are good conductors of heat and electric current. (See also alloy.)

▲ Plastic is a type of **material**.

▼ If metal becomes hot enough, it will **melt**.

mineral A material that is mined, or dug from the ground.

moisture Wetness, or dampness.

Moon The Moon orbits the Earth. Unlike the Earth, it does not rotate, so it always has the same side facing Earth. It looks bright because the Sun is shining on it. The changing shape of the bright area is caused by the Earth blocking the Sun's light and making a shadow on the Moon. (See also gravity, moonlight, night and weight.)

moonlight Light that comes from the Sun but is reflected off the Moon.

move (moving) An object moves, or shows movement or motion, as a result of a force, such as gravity, acting on it. All moving objects have kinetic energy.

natural Made by nature, not manufactured.

newton Forces are measured in newtons. The stronger the push or pull, the greater the number of newtons. It takes a force of about 1 newton to lift a small apple. An object with a mass of 1 kilogram has a weight of 10 newtons.

▲ The Sun is shining on part of the **Moon**.

▲ The force needed to lift a small apple is about 1 **newton**.

night

night The time between sunset and sunrise. (See also day and Earth.)

non-magnetic A way of describing something that is not attracted to a magnet.

o

opaque Does not let light pass through. (See also translucent and transparent.)

optical To do with light and seeing.

orbit Keep travelling around an object, especially an object in space, following a circle-like path.

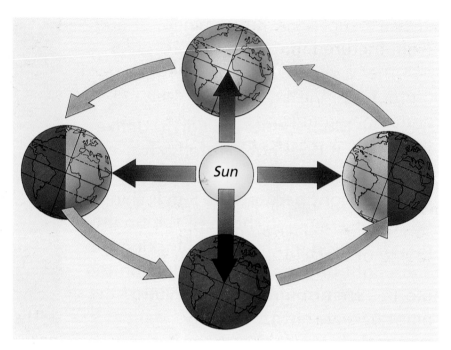

Sun

▲ The Earth **orbits** the Sun.

p

parallel circuit A circuit that has more than one way, or path, for the electric current to go. Even if one part of one path in a parallel circuit stops working, the current will still flow around another path. (See also series circuit.)

particle Everything is made up of very tiny parts. These are known as particles.

▲ The bulb nearest the battery in this **parallel circuit** will work even if the path to the second is broken.

plastic Plastics are a group of manufactured materials that includes polythene, nylon and PVC. They are very useful materials because they are light and strong and can be made into any shape. Most plastics are electrical insulators.

plug A special fitting that is used to connect an electrical machine to a source of electricity through a socket.

pole The ends of a magnet are called the poles. They are where the magnet's magnetic force is the strongest. Every magnet has two poles. One is called the north pole and the other the south pole. (See also attract and repel.)

potential energy A type of energy that is stored up, ready to be used. Potential energy often changes into kinetic energy. Anything that has been stretched, squeezed or wound up has potential energy. When it is let go, it moves. Anything that is above the Earth's surface also has potential energy. It moves when it falls to the ground as a result of gravity. (See also chemical energy.)

powder A dust-like substance, usually made by grinding or crushing a solid.

▲ These coconuts have **potential energy**.

▲ The paper clips are attracted to this magnet's **poles**.

power station

power station A place where electricity is made. It can then be moved along cables to the places where it is to be used.

prism A transparent object that can be used to spread, or break up, light into a spectrum of colours. Raindrops can act like prisms to produce a rainbow.

property To do with describing or measuring particular things about a material. The properties of the metal copper, for instance, include being good at conducting heat and electric current and having a melting point of 1083 degrees Celsius. The particular properties of a material will make it suitable for particular uses.

pulley A wheel with a piece of rope or cable wound round it. When one end of the rope is pulled, any objects attached to the other end of the rope are lifted up. More wheels and rope can be added to lift heavier loads. The pulley is a type of simple machine.

pylon A tall object, made of metal, that is used to hold up cables that carry electric current from power stations.

q

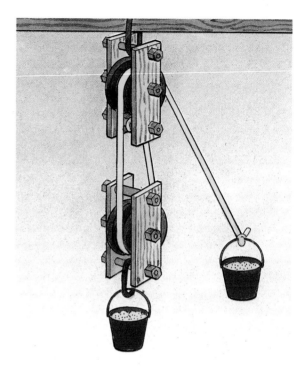

▲ This is a **pulley**.

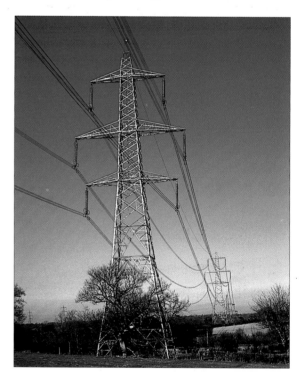

▲ **Pylons** hold up cables that carry electricity.

r

ramp Also called slope or inclined plane. It is a type of simple <u>machine</u>. It is easier to push something up a slope than it is to lift it straight up. However, the distance it has to travel is longer.

ray A line of <u>light</u>.

reaction See <u>chemical reaction</u>.

reflect Send back or <u>bounce</u> back <u>light</u>, <u>heat</u> or <u>sound</u>.

repel Push away. When a <u>magnet</u> pushes another magnet away, it is said to be repelling that magnet. Two magnets will repel each other if they have the same <u>poles</u> facing each other. (See also <u>attract</u>.)

resistance To do with <u>particles</u> within a <u>wire</u> or other object slowing down <u>electric current</u> as it flows through. (See also <u>air resistance</u>.)

reversible Can change, or be changed, back to the way it was.

rigid Cannot bend or be bent. Not <u>flexible</u>.

rotate Spin around a centre or turning point.

rough Feels uneven or bumpy. Not <u>smooth</u>.

▲ Moonlight is sunlight that is **reflected** off the Moon.

▼ A globe **rotates** in the same way the Earth does.

scale

scale To do with measuring things. A scale is made up of equal steps, or units, that can be counted. (See also Celsius and Fahrenheit.)

screw A type of simple machine. It works like a wrapped up ramp. Screws have to be turned.

series circuit A circuit that is made up of one loop. It may have more than one battery or light bulb or switch but there is only one way, or path, for the electric current to take.
If there is a break in any part of a series circuit, the current will not flow. (See also parallel circuit.)

shadow An area of darkness that is caused by something opaque blocking light. Light can only travel in straight lines, so it cannot reach the area that is being blocked.

shiny The opposite of dull. A shiny material reflects light very well.

sink Be pulled down by gravity through a material, such as water or air. An object continues to sink until it reaches something that will hold it up, such as the ground.

slope See ramp.

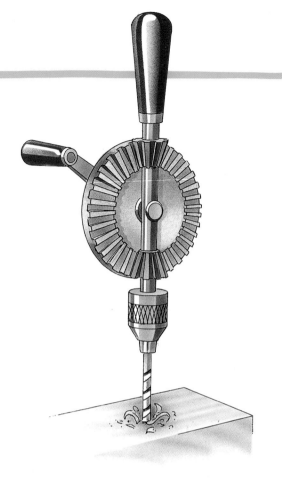

▲ This hand drill uses the idea of a **screw**.

▲ This is a **series circuit**.

smooth Feels even, without any bumps. Not rough.

soak Make very wet. Or, make a material take in as much liquid as it can.

socket A special fitting that is used to connect a plug to a source of electricity.

soft Will give when touched or pressed. The opposite of hard.

solid One of the three states of matter. A solid cannot flow. Its volume cannot be changed. It has a shape that usually stays the same. Solids are often hard.

soluble Able to be dissolved.

solution A mixture made up of a liquid with something dissolved in it.

▲ This jug is a **solid**.

sound A type of energy. A sound is made when something vibrates. The thing that is vibrating makes the air around it start to vibrate. The vibrations in the air spread out, rather like the ripples you see when you throw a stone into a pond. When the vibrating air reaches your ear it makes liquid in your ear vibrate and you hear the sound. The loudness of sound is measured in decibels. (See also conductor and insulator.)

▲ **Sounds** make the air vibrate.

source

source Where something comes from.

spectrum The band of colours that a ray of light can be split into, especially by using a prism. As a ray of light travels through a prism, the light is bent. Some colours bend more than others and so the colours become spread out.

speed How fast something moves. Speed is usually measured in kilometres per hour or miles per hour.

squash Squeeze or press to make smaller or flatter.

states of matter Different forms of a material.
There are three states: liquid, solid and gas. Water, for example, is in its liquid state when it comes out of the tap. When it is frozen, it is in its solid state and is called ice. When it boils or evaporates it becomes a type of gas called water vapour.

static electricity See electricity.

steel Any of a group of alloys that are mostly made up of iron. It includes stainless steel.

stretch Make longer, wider or bigger, often by pulling.

▲ Rainbows show the different colours of the **spectrum**.

▲ The liquid state is one of the **states of matter**.

stretchy Able to be stretched.

substance Type of material.

Sun A large object made up of burning gases. The Sun is a star. The Earth orbits around the Sun. It is our main source of energy and gives out both light and heat. (See also gravity.)

surface Either the outside or the top of something.

switch Switches are used to turn things on and off. A switch usually includes a piece of metal. When the switch is moved, it makes the piece of metal move too. This completes or breaks the electrical circuit.

synthetic Describes a material that has been built up by chemical reactions. Nylon is a synthetic material. Also often used to mean manufactured, or not natural.

t

temperature How hot or cold something is. Temperature is measured in degrees, using a thermometer. (See also Celsius and Fahrenheit.)

▲ The **Sun** gives out light and heat.

▲ A **switch** is used to turn this torch on and off.

texture

texture The feel of something. Rough and smooth are examples of words that can be used to describe texture.

thermometer An instrument that is used to measure temperature. (See also Celsius and Fahrenheit.)

translucent Lets some light pass through but is not transparent. (See also opaque.)

transparent Lets light pass through. (See also opaque and translucent.)

▲ Sunglasses are **translucent**.

▼ This glass is **transparent**.

u

v

vibrate Wobble backwards and forwards very quickly.

visible Can be seen.

volume The amount of space something takes up. It is not the same as its mass. Mass cannot change but the volume of some things, such as gases, can change as a result of being heated or compressed.
Can also be used to mean the loudness of sound.

W

water cycle Water <u>evaporates</u> from the land, the sea and rivers and becomes <u>water vapour</u> in the air. The water vapour <u>condenses</u> to form clouds, then falls to the <u>Earth</u> as rain or snow and the cycle starts all over again.

water vapour The form that water takes when it <u>boils</u> or <u>evaporates</u> and becomes a <u>gas</u>.

waterproof Will not let <u>water</u> pass through.

weigh <u>Measure</u> the <u>mass</u> (not the <u>weight</u>) of something.

weight To do with how heavy something is. The weight of something depends on how strong the pull of <u>gravity</u> on it is. An object has more weight on the <u>Earth</u> than it does on the <u>Moon</u> because the pull of gravity on the Earth is greater than on the Moon. Weight is a <u>force</u>, so it is <u>measured</u> in <u>newtons</u>. (See also <u>mass</u> and <u>weigh</u>.)

wire A long, thin thread of <u>metal</u>.

snow falls

rain falls

clouds form

evaporation

evaporation

water flows back into the sea

▲ The **water cycle**.

▲ Water turns to **water vapour** when it boils.

Index

The numbers that are printed in **bold** show the pages of the main explanations.
The numbers that are printed in *italics* show the pages where there are pictures.

A word may appear in more than one explanation on any one page.